I0622789

YOUR TRUE ESSENCE
FREQUENCIES OF THE NEW WORLD
BOOK ONE

CORYNTHIA SOUL ASCENDER

YOUR TRUE ESSENCE

CONTENTS

INTRODUCTION

These series of books are for those who are ready to let go of the reins and open to all possibilities of experience. Receive this information with love and gratitude. This book is for the masses. The information upon these written pages holds all the frequencies of this New World. Those who read it will receive these frequencies. It will create an ease in this lifetime for each individual, with a new journey being created on each level of experience.

Channeled directly from the Council of Twelve Arcturians—there is rhythm and rhyme to each of these words as they may not be spoken in the traditional way. Know that each word carries a certain sound, vibration and frequency that enters into the mind and on all levels of the body. This allows the mind to recalculate its beliefs, its knowings, and ideas. What we refer to as "all levels of the body" does not mean just the physical. It permeates the soul and all the energy around it. Your growth of frequency allows the expansion of consciousness on a universal level, allowing others to feel this frequency as well.

LIFE

*W*hat is life and why is there life?

Good questions. Life is simply an experience to evolve each soul into an experience that was not available before. How? Through the simple things of emotions, sensations, experimentation, and creation. It feels tough because it was to toughen each individual in order to bring forward a new evolved world for themself and to better the world around them.

Life is the answer for soul achievement. Create the knowing from within. Do not allow the world to shut you down and make you fit into the ego's idea as it is not your illusion but theirs they have created to control you. Do not feel you are unworthy as this is a falsity that has been created to keep you in place of their control. Release what you think you know and allow the new and full truth to enter. There is no one but you. There is no thing but you. It is your time to claim that. If you do not claim that someone else will and will decide your life for you. You have the power to claim what it is that your soul is here to learn in this life. Do not doubt your abilities and capabilities. You all have them deep within and just need to be re-awakened to bring forward the true purpose of the soul. The soul is much more than the mind thinks it knows of it. The soul is unable to die. The soul is the vessel to embody all bodies to have an experience. The soul is the truth and the experience of all.

Read the signs of feeling within the body and it will lead you on a path of experience with much more ease and understanding. You do not need to stay in the mud as it is your own creation. Create the mud with the beauty it truly is and the ease to walk through it without worry of needing to go around it. Mud is only what you choose to perceive it as. Release that part within and see it as the fun it can be.

Life is your expression. Do not allow others beliefs and ideas to keep you from expressing yourself. Be clear and into all that is of what you want. Feel deep beyond your heart. Feel deep into every particle of your being. This is creation.

AWAKEN

*T*his journey of life is no longer what you think it is. We have purposefully kept one eye closed to understanding your true being because you are limited to the human experience. The experiment is now over. This will take years to unravel and come into balance once again. The souls upon this earth are now leaving to go back to where they came from. Think of this life as a board game of chess. Many have played for many lifetimes. We see the clarity of this experiment and it is time to rewrite and recreate it so we no longer lose sight of what this experiment was always meant to be. Some souls do not want to stop playing as they have completely forgotten who they once were. Those are the ones that will continue on their own timeline and delusional illusional world. As for the rest of the game, it is now coming to an end to rewrite it in love and light. Life should have always been with the respect for the world you live upon.

As you all awake with both of your eyes open to all aspects of our being, down to the cells and their cells, you will feel and know the truth. All else will fall away. As the clarity comes through for each one of you, it may take time to implement and reprogram the mind to open up to levels it has never opened up to before. As you let go of the old and continue to receive the light of knowing, the cells will open up and recreate this existence. This is new to this world. This is new to humans. And it is even new to all those ascended here that are to create the New World. This frequency is a collaboration of all beings and all worlds together. This is the first time we have all come together in this capacity creating the new experience and experiment of being able to be in human form. There may be times that it feels like life is failing but, as this is new to you, it is new to us, too. Remember there is no such thing as failing, this is not a word of truth, as you have not done something that keeps you from being the extraordinary being that you are. It is purely an experiment. It is simply recreating, recreating, and recreating so you are in the time dimension of self expression of all its beauty, all its joy, and all its pain in a way that it is understandable.

The experiences of your life allow you to be able to navigate this world in a much easier way than humans have chosen to do in the past. None of these experiences are to destroy a soul. All of this is to help elevate our consciousness, not just humans but, all intergalactically. Through the expression of a human being we are able to experience things that our light bodies currently cannot experience. Those of you that are light beings in a human form are here not only to experience this humanness but to experience the part of you that is us - in all ways. As a collaboration, we can create the human form into the light being that we are with the sensations of being a human. This is the experiment. It was never meant to go as dark as it has gone with confusion and chaos. This aspect has become important because you do not know the light unless you know the dark. The light is what is

4

to become. The dark is a choice and it's okay too. We do not want to continue this continuum of light and dark separation, chaos or cruelty. We have adjusted so that Gaia moves forward with the beings that have chosen to be in the light. Those who do not want to awaken or choose love, humility, and humbleness of this earth will choose their own earth. It can play out as the individuals may choose. As each soul chooses to transform, they need to ascend. They may call it heaven, they may call it anything else but, ultimately it is transforming into the 5th of where the true Gaia exist now.

Gaia was never here to be abused as it is its own being. Yes, it has the capability of wiping all human beings in existence out, but that is not what the goal is. The goal is to proceed in a loving, gentle, respectful manner for all types of beings of all walks of life, and to live in this peaceful, harmonious way of give and take in a beautiful, comforting, solid way.

There are some beings that are going to be teachers to teach others to walk upon Gaia in a much different way. But it does not mean they're any better than anyone else. It just purely is their role upon the earth. As all men, women, and children and every living creature on the earth has a reciprocal role of uniting and joining together in a harmonious way.

Each being brings forward an amazing aspect of its own. No one and no thing is less than or more than. Each piece is important. It is all your choice of how you choose to create this life in your mind and in your heart and in all aspects of your human self. Our goal is to get you to feel complete and to be able to work through all the soul's evolution of transformation with much more ease. Do not feel this is a burden. As this is a journey of recreating the human aspect, in the human mind and the human body, with integration of all the light beings that you are.

ENSLAVEMENT

We give you all the admiration, all the love, for you choosing to be in this lifetime at this time. We know this is not an easy existence. As what was normal is no longer and it will never be again. The direction that each of you were going was not a direction that will continue the life cycle of humans in a positive way. It was literally destroying each one of you even though you may have thought you were okay. Life is not what it was and we no longer can allow it to continue in that direction. You've chosen to come into this body, in this lifetime, to help transform the world into a direction that is sustainable for life creating what it was always meant to be.

Life is simply an experience and experiment created in an illusion. The illusion is what allows you to create whatever path you choose to want to walk. Nothing is right or wrong as it is your game to navigate. No one or nothing can affect it the way you can. You were given an opportunity not to remember so that you can experience all of the humanness of what human is. Now is the time that we awaken each one of you. It is ultimately up to you to want this awakening. It is not right or wrong what you're choosing. That is the agreement being in the human body.

For us, we are here to guide you to the evolution of what you have chosen to create while embodying this body. Not one of you is alone. As you feel you are only human, you feel very alone. It is our duty to help awaken and introduce you to your others, who are like you. You are here to continue evolving and to continue the evolution of this world. Each being has a mission.

Some of you know where your soul is from. Many, many do not and that's perfect. As this is not their time to be conflicted with more conflict of confusion. Simply be your true being, standing centered in your power, and this will help others to awaken. Be patient, do not force, do not manipulate, just allow. Your light in your frequency, in that expansion of love, radiates from all aspects of your body and will affect everything. Everything! Creating a new direction and a new evolution of what this world is to be.

It's been said that light has already won. In some aspects this is true. In other aspects human beings still ultimately have choices where they may choose differently. The light has not already won. The light is currently strengthening and creating the new change in the direction of the earth so it may be at peace once again.

Earth was never meant to be mutilated, disrespected, and destroyed. Somehow by losing your true identity (soul self) human's evolution has felt that it's okay. We are here to regain respect upon this earth and with all living beings. No matter how big or how small. Do not be angry with yourself for the disrespect. As ultimately most of us, most of you, did not know better. But now that you are aware, it's a choice. As the new children step into this world they do remember, they do know. They are here to replant and repot all that is needed for this earth to thrive once again.

Humans are to be light beings in the human body while thriving. They are not to be enslaved by all the world's ideas, beliefs, and ultimate captivation of greed. You were never meant to be a slave of anyone or anything. Unfortunately, as evolution continued you have learned to enslave yourself. These belief systems will now be broken, changed, and transmuted thus, allowing the truth of what is possible to be brought into you.

Once again it does come down to choice, as that is the agreement in human form. The ideas and belief systems that have created enslavement in humans have made humans think that they're not worthy and they're less than. They have to strive so hard as to "break their back" to continue to create this "belief system." This is not real! There's no aspect of it that is real. Those that you look up to, it's not real. They are just as broken. They have learned to deceive, manipulate, and create this illusion of untruth. The absolute truth is within you. You need to go inward, centering into who you are, and allowing your cells to resonate with the information that you feel buzzing inside you. Bring this forward with all its scariness, grief, intensity and emotions. Bringing it forward to allow it to become what is you. Nothing, no one, or no belief system can destroy you if you stand in that power. That power is you! You do not need to enslave, harm or manipulate yourself or anyone to get to that power.

Financial idea of abundance is not truth. Money was never meant to be what it has become of ugliness, greediness, destroying others, and destroying yourself to get it. That's the enslavement. This enslavement must end! Power in your world means financial abundance and control. True power is not that. Ultimately, you are the power and you can create this world and any illusion you choose when you let go of this "belief system."

IDENTITY

*D*o not allow other ideas and belief systems, that do not feel like your truth, to become your truth. There are many ideas and many ways that things are being done out there. There are not necessarily wrong or right ways but there are paths that are going to keep you from being your full potential. Do not place yourself in any type of box or under any title, as this is simply the ego wanting to belong. Do not force or create ideas that make you feel you belong. You belong! Humanity is notorious for this. It is time for you to be okay with no title, no box and no method. You must release thought patterns of "this is how it has to be" or "that's the only way;" otherwise, you're completely limiting yourself from fully stepping in. These ideas have kept many healers throughout the centuries from becoming actually what they were meant to be.

Your identity is unique as each soul comes from different places and has its own uniqueness and own experiences before receiving itself into the human body. Some souls have been around many lifetimes, some are new. A new soul doesn't mean that you're a newborn soul, it simply means that you're new upon this earth as a human being. Each soul has evolved in its own ways and is at different levels.

Your identity of who or what you think you are will dissipate quickly or slowly as you transition into your awakening. That is part of your journey. We allowed each of you the time and challenge to experience being human with no or little remembrance of who you really are. Transitioning into your new identity is not something that you need to do or create as it already is implemented inside your cells and DNA. It is now being awakened and blossoming like a flower from within. Your true self has always been in your body, it has just been dormant. This transformation is not a hostile takeover or a walk in, it is simply you growing into you. The time has come for you to be called into the mastery and work that you're here to do. You do still have the choice to follow through or not follow through. But those of you that are here for the bigger purpose, we will create life in a way to nudge you into following your true path. Otherwise, life will not be fun. Your humanness will still be there but, you will see life in a very different way. Life will not be in the way that you currently experience it. It will be in a way that you are able to do your work without the attachments, pain or suffering that you endured before. You're not actually leaving this world but, transitioning this world. It will come with you or you go with it later, depending on the timeline that you transition.

All of you are here to be teachers to help others as they also choose to awaken. Each awakening of humankind will be on their timeline and level. Just as it was for you. A lot of you are on a fast track of awakening. Some of you already understand and know this consciously as well as your cells and soul. You are simply stepping into it. You have been called now to fully awaken into the power you are so you can help us transition this world into the 5th. Your identity will continue to slip away from your ego mind of this human existence. Do not be sad or feel that you're going crazy. Do not feel that there's something wrong with your mind. No longer will you be activated through the mind but will be activated through the heart. As you step into this, the world will seem extremely different from how you interact and are part of it. Do not be afraid as this is your mission of why you are here upon this earth at this time. There are many, many of you on this earth in this timeline to create the New World. Each one of you has your own group. There are multiple different types of beings that are helping with this. This is a new challenge and a new way of life for human beings. Do not be discouraged. We are here in all the ways possible to work alongside you for this transformation for yourself and the world.

Losing your many aspects of your current human identity is safe and okay. It is all part of the plan. It is part of the sacrifice and leveling up so that we can make this New World happen. You will know exactly who you are prior to being in this new human body. You will know it, you will feel it, it will be you. You will feel comfort with that. Allow this to happen. Once again do not be afraid of this. Some aspects will still be you, just a much more amazing version of you. You'll be the teachers to guide the humans and other existences into the New World.

BODY

*I*t is now time to recreate the body as one whole being versus separation of my arm, my foot, my head, my eye - things like that. Human beings are so notorious for creating separation within their own human body. It is time that you create the body as one whole. There is no separation from you and your soul provided you are embodying your body with all its potential. The soul has to step out once in a while, as it needs to do its soul work upon this earth. This should not negatively affect you in a way that you are not able to be in your whole being in this bodily world.

The body that you live in is a perfected machine. It has a perfected blue print that is capable of reforming and redesigning constantly. As you learn to fully embody your body with your soul, the soul will teach the body and its cells to recreate itself in a magnificent, perfected way. You will be able to live in an upgraded way and no longer be limited as you have experienced in the past. The hardest concept for humans to understand is that the mind actually creates the physical on many levels. Not only is it just your mind but also your heart and other aspects of your life that you create. For this perfection it may not be possible in this particular lifetime but that is what we're attempting to do. As you transition into the 5th dimension it allows the body to understand this concept in a much better way. You will be able to physically, and in every aspect emotionally, recreate the body in the way that is perfected for you.

The perfection that you desire tends to be on shallow levels as this is not what the body was meant for. The perfection we are talking about is perfection of a body to live in harmony with all its surroundings. As this is not something we can explain at this time for you to fully understand. Just understand that this body is much more than you can fathom. You need to treat it with all the respect that you possibly can. Do not be angry at yourself for not knowing better. This is a new challenge and a new journey. We ask that you fully embrace this. Enjoy the expectations of exploration of this new found concept within your physical body.

SOUL

*E*xperiences are necessary for the change of what the soul wants to ultimately learn and receive in this human form. Know that all souls have chosen to play this lifetime out with you regardless of how hard it may feel.

Every soul has a different mission. Each soul is working upon this earth, knowing it or not. It is the soul's progressive challenge to create and recreate what is going on in this exact plane so that the world's existence can contain and maintain itself. At all times your soul is a wise and knowing being. Some souls are younger but it does not mean that they are unwise. It's just younger in the essence of this particular world. It is not younger in other worlds.

The new children that are coming into this world have souls that are highly evolved. They understand much more than most of the current souls on this earth. These souls are here to be the new beginning and procreating the new human being. These souls are the souls that are going to help up-level the world of the older souls. They will allow you to see this version of the world in a very different way.

Souls have a purpose. Do not underestimate the soul. Do

not underestimate the physical being that your soul is in. As this is all to be transformed and evolved into one. When you die in this world your soul will continue to evolve. No soul is actually lost, at least permanently. Some souls may choose to be lost for a short while upon the earthly planes. It may not go where you think it should go. It will go to the next evolutionary step of where that soul has chosen to recreate and relive its ideas of what it would like to learn. That means it may come back to this earthly plane or go back to its home planetary system or might evolve into a different planetary system. None of you are from one particular place. Many of you have traveled and lived in many different existences upon the galaxies at large. The galaxies out there are way beyond your human mind's ability to understand. As you get to learn more and more about the different astrological areas and different galaxies out there, your brain still has a hard time conceptualizing. You are not the only beings in this world or universe. As that would be a very small, limited space. There are many, many different types of beings and they're from all walks, different earths and different galaxies. Some are not of the highest vibrational ideas of how to live and some are very highly evolved into the light, as you so call it. But there is nothing wrong with any of it as it is its own individual growth.

HEART

*T*he heart energy is centered in the middle of the chest. The heart energy is the true mind. The heart is what connects the soul into the body. Each heart has been tarnished and has been through so much. It is time now to allow the heart to be cleaned, opened and ready to receive all aspects of your true being. Envision the heart is the true cord that connects you to the human body with the soul. Without the heart, the soul no longer contains itself within this existence of a human body. Your heart when fully expanded and opened will affect all aspects of your physical being. It creates healing, clarity and true vision of the truth of this world and how to navigate it with ease. The expanded heart is the true expansion of your whole being. This is what you all are and to become in the 5th. This is the key. This transition will not happen without the heart being fully expanded, centered and locked in with the soul. If mankind tries to only use their mind it will not happen, as the mind creates all reality of non-truths. The heart is the only truth.

Envision your chest cavity expanding now. Allowing all aspects of your heart to be seen. Allow each edge of your heart energy to be softened, yet strong. Allow yourself to see everything that is going on in that area. There are many memories and many ideas that have been placed inside there. Go through the heart and unlock each of those doors. You may step in if you choose or just look through. Allow your heart to be released from all of these. Clear out and integrate these memories and ideas in a way that is emotionless and non-attached. Fill these spaces with true love. What we mean by true love is love of self and love of all in acceptance with no judgment toward yourself or anything else. Now allow yourself to release the emotions attached with love and acceptance. While doing this be in a surrendered state of receiving and gratitude for all you have experienced. These experiences are for your personal growth.

Loving yourself is probably one of the hardest aspects of transformation each human will go through. Loving yourself has very rarely been taught correctly or thoroughly. Unfortunately, it has been taught in a way as being narcissistic or selfish. This is not true of you. True love of self is standing in your full power. No judgment while receiving all that is. Walking through this world in unity with all. This concept is hard to understand, as this will be the new existence of humans in the 5th. It is difficult to do this as you currently walk upon this earth. It will continue to become clearer and make sense as the world transitions.

The heart will go through multiple transformations. As each layer is released and opened up, the heart will feel safer and more secure. The heart transformation can be physically painful. Your rib cage and sternum may experience pain as the area physically and emotionally opens up. It will hold energy differently than it ever has. The heart itself may feel like a muscle that has not been used in a very long time and you can experience pain within and around it. Do not be concerned as this is not dangerous or something that is wrong with you. Your heart is meant to be opened and expanded. Many humans have only experienced closed-off, sunken-in and contracted hearts. As your heart expands and opens and you learn to truly love yourself, it may be the most painful experience you've ever had in "love."

Learning to love yourself on a level you've never known expands you to a completely new frequency. Release the pain that you and the world has brought upon your heart with no judgment. The heart has to be healed to move forward and it can only be healed within yourself by acceptance. Acceptance that you are perfect in all your "flaws." The perfection of being human and all that is.

The heart will breathe on its own and resonate a frequency higher and higher as you learn to continue to expand in your healing. Others will feel this expansion of love that is coming from you through their heart. It is much more potent than anything else you can do. As your heart allows this new frequency to permeate in and around it, unconsciously other beings will experience the higher frequency. Helping them to choose to raise their own.

As your heart opens up there's a glow that radiates the true inner beauty of your power. This will permeate your outer shell. The heart is not as complicated as you may think. It is simply like a wounded animal that needs trust, fed positive energy, releasing without torture of self judgement, knowing that it is loved and never alone. For the heart to know its true strength and power, it needs to be fully opened and be the center of all things.

MIND

This is a tricky subject as all we know is our mind. That's how we have survived over thousands and thousands of years of humanity. We lose touch of our knowing and our wisdom within ourselves. The wisdom that is literally embedded in your DNA in cells. The wisdom of the heart being in control. We've created the mind almost as a separate part of our being. We have both the good and the bad aspects of the mind. The devil and the angel on the shoulder - attitude within the mind. The mind has been so perfected in a way of making it be in control that within an instant, it can destroy all that is perfect. All that is divine. All that is the amazing beauty of this human form. The mind is now the instrument of control in most humans and creates conflict in your reality. It is important to allow yourself the opportunity to expand the mind into what is possible.

It is time to drop the mind from that pedestal and to make it be in balance, on an even playing field with the rest of your being. The key to doing this is not to condemn your mind (or those that call it ego) rather, love it, thank it, be in complete gratitude for why it's there. Ask it nicely, "Hey, we're a team. Thank you for all the hard work you've done but, let's rest awhile. Let's take a break. You will not be pushed out. As I always will need you. But, right now let's be calm and quiet so that we can engage the heart with each moment, each breath and each thought." That way the heart can be a team with the mind as one. As you engage the heart it engages the whole part of you that has been absent in this lifetime and possibly many, many lifetimes.

Drop the energy into the heart center. Drop down into the pelvis. Drop down into the earth. Then come from the earth back through to the heart. Then bring the energy up through the throat and into the mind. Allow the energy to go beyond the top of your head. This will give you a center balance of pulling your power force and source in the energy of perfection. The mind is to be a tool of the heart. To perform through pure intentions that come from the heart while being grounded into your body and grounded into this earth. The mind is magnificent. Many humans have zero understanding of how magnificently and massively the mind can create your reality. If you harness your mind in a way of positivity, of being engaged through and by the heart only, your mind will literally, physically expand. This will allow you to use your whole brain, your whole mind, your whole embodiment that the mind is encased with. This is where humans are to go into. You're not just a physical form. As each thought that passes through the mind creates a frequency of some sort. Some frequencies will land where intended to, some will dissipate, some will randomly hit beings or things. So we want the mind to become the part of your heart that is of pure intention. You can use this for good or bad, so be conscientious of how you're creating thoughts.

The goal is to drop everything first into the heart and then bring it up into the mind to express. The mind is very beautiful. It is very intense. It is extremely useful if we learn to use it in a proper and positive way. It will create a life of much more ease for those of you that struggle with a mind that constantly chews up, regurgitates, rethinks things, creates its own agenda, and does whatever it thinks it wants to do. No pun intended. Allow the mind to be the instrument. The instrument that plays out actions from the heart.

BREATH

*B*reath of the body. There are a lot of ideas of what breath means. Breath of the body means draw inward, bringing all the energy into a center core then dropping down into the earth. Allowing that breath to not only go all the way into the earth but also, all the way up into the heavens. Creating the center axis of your body. The breath that you draw inward into the body keeps us pulled together energetically, similar to a corset being synched up. Breath is also used to expel things. So you can draw in and breathe it out of anything that no longer serves you. Breath is powerful. Breath brings you to you.

No matter what the situation is, breath gives you that space and time, which is only on this earth, to reevaluate, to reclaim and to transform. Breath even in its quickness can be an infinite amount of time to transform anything. Transform your beliefs that you may have. Transform any energy that may have been placed upon you. Transform thoughts that are not of the highest vibration. Breath is the key to it all.

Breath is essential for all healing of the body. Being aware of your depths of breath and the strength of each breath can tell you a lot of what is going on in the unconscious and within your physical being. Breath work is essential for releasing stuck and stagnant energy and bringing in the new energy of life. With breath comes taste and smell for a more in depth experience of this human existence.

VOICE

*Y*our voice is an intricate part of your expression. The voice carries frequencies that will permeate all things if used correctly. Through your voice, your words, your intentions, the vibrations can be felt around the universe. Through your voice you are able to stand on your own as the power house you are. Through your voice you can create anything. The key to understanding your voice is realizing that the voice needs to come from the heart. Through the heart the voice is robust and potent. Do not be a voice from the mind or a voice on its own. The voice from there is emptiness. It needs to be grounded into the heart and up into the throat and brought through the mouth. You can land a vibration of intention without even saying the words. The vibration can come through with just a single tone. The voice allows you to set your boundaries so that you can stand in your strength and not be blown away by others. Your voice is something to be respected, to be loved, to be playful and to be out there in a way of positive change. Allow your voice to be everything.

But know that your voice is only as strong as you allow the intention coming from the heart to flow through. The heart is the true strength of your voice.

HEAL

$\mathcal{T}$he key to healing yourself is through the heart. Feel the energy within your heart of pure and nonjudgmental love. Allow it to expand and strengthen. Breathe into it. Then you bring the energy down or up into whatever area of the body that needs healing. Envision that area to be a sick or injured animal. Feel the love you want to give it to take it out of pain. The love you want to give it to help it to be happy and comfortable. Bring that same beautiful love right into yourself. Envision the illness or injury literally healing, closing up and expelling out of the body.

Understand that the illness or injury does not exist on a level we believe it does. A lot of times, especially with disease or illness, it is a whole collaboration of ideas that have been squashed down and not released like guilt, shame, pain or trauma. This build up of the energy field will create the emotions into the physical to let you know it needs to be addressed. Allow the emotions to open up and be loved by you and released out. The disease and illness will dissipate rapidly if done correctly and thoroughly. Regarding direct physical injuries, it most of the time carries emotional elements that have not been addressed and will continue to surface. Other times, physical injuries are simply a wake up call or to take us in a different direction. Some injuries and illnesses are a contract we made before entering into this human body to teach us lessons or is meant to be the end of this life-cycle.

You must take care of the physical body as it needs pure nourishment. Not only emotionally and of clear mind but, with healthy, organic, well treated, respected and with gratitude food. Your body needs particular nutrients to live in this existence. You must look at your body as a temple. A temple that is housing your soul so that you can have the most magnificent possibilities of living in this journey. When the physical body is ill it is very difficult to pull out of that state because all you can feel is that pain. The way to step out of that pain is to allow your soul to be released out the body on some level. Place your soul and body energetically into your happy space, safe space, comfortable space, wherever that is. Allowing your soul to engage in whatever fun it wants to have while being there with your body. Telling your body "thank you" for how magnificent it is. Loving your body as if you would love anybody else. Being there and supporting your body. Telling your body to forgive you for all the pain and suffering you've created. Telling your body you love it. Engage with your body, with all the nourishment possible, on every level.

When it comes to healing the physical body you need to be there giving it the nutrients, oxygen, sun, fresh air and water. Otherwise, the body gets stagnant and is not able to release with ease whatever is creating the illness or injury. Continually envision that part of you that needs healing, healing and healed. If there is anything that's attached into that area, be there with it as if you're listening to a sick, injured child. Ask it "What is it that I need to know?" "What do I need to hear?" "What do I need to help you through this?" "What can we do as a team to get you healthy again with strength and vitality?" Listen to your body. Be there with your body. Be patient with your body. Be without judgment with anything that comes up. As that judgment will not allow it to surface and be released. All healing is possible. Healing is being there as one unit with pure compassion, love and non-judgment.

So often there is so much buried within you, down to your cellular level, that you are unaware of. Some of it could have been handed down from generation to generation. It could have been placed upon you from the pollution in the world, pollution of what you hear, see or feel. Allow that to come forward. Whatever comes forward does not make you in any way a bad person or for you to feel shameful or guilty.

Being human is literally being part of a system to feel all spectrums of what being human is. From being painful to being happy and joyful. Allow this to come through. Allow the tears to shed and the anger to come forward or whatever it is emotionally that wants to come through. Allow it. Just be there with it just like you would with anybody else. Just love it and thank it and forgive it and tell it "Wow! You are so strong for showing up while bringing to me what I need to know so that we can as one become stronger." Be there for your body. Be what you would want someone else to be for you. Be aware that there is so much unknown trapped within your body that it just needs to be heard, loved, and released. When you do this, some of this is from your DNA and past heritage, you have not just healed your own but your past lineage of that particular thing. Feel honored you are strong enough to endure whatever it was you had to endure to release and heal this.

You were never given anything more than what you can handle. Even if life feels like it needs to end now. Just breathe it in. Recognize this is more than just you. Recognize you have the power to open this up and let it go. Then you will start to see happiness shining through.

As I've said in previous chapters, you cannot understand the light if you haven't endured some of the dark. Unfortunately, a lot of us healers of the world have to endure a lot of dark to endure a lot of light. That is human experience and in all its perfection that it is.

RELEASE

*T*here are so many ideas of what release means. All are correct on their own level.

It can be difficult to release your human self of all the ideas that have been embedded, created and pressed upon you. As it has created a cage so thick and dense you have forgotten what the sunlight looks like. When you allow yourself to release, each of you will do it in a different way. There is no right way of doing it except for what is right for you. For some, release may come crashing through or come with ease. It may be slow or rapid. It is all positive. As you release you will experience all the emotions trapped inside. Each emotion has its own story. Some stories just need to be heard. Not by other human beings but by yourself. It needs to be felt, loved, held, respected and then brought into a loving light. As you draw that story into your heart, that's where the true release is.

Due to the dense human experience, there are many, many stories in each of our bodies. As the stories are built upon stories, upon stories, with no energy release from them, they eventually crush the body and the soul. When the soul doesn't want to stay in the body due to too much pain of any sort, it will exit the body on different levels. If the soul is not seated in the body, the body will start deteriorating. Deterioration of your body is due to the soul escaping. "It just feels so heavy, so hard." As you choose to bring your soul back into the physical form, the body heals. The body is the casing for the soul. So when the soul is doing what is meant to do with all its glory, the body heals miraculously, if that's what you want to call it.

The soul is wise. Some souls are more evolved and some aren't. It does not mean that they're any different than you. Each soul has come into this human body form to perform a duty. This could mean playing the bad guy or good guy role or whatever story it wants to play out. It is meant to be here. Once again, you do not know the light if you do not know the dark. You must have a way to see the contrast and see the difference between. So embrace the darkness as if it is the light, love it. Know that you have all sides within you in this human form. There's nothing to be ashamed of, as this is human experience.

As you raise your shadows or if you want to call them skeletons, out of your darkness, embrace and love them just like they are a light being. Be there with them and then release them into the heart with acceptance. All the traumas and all the injustice that happened with you, love them. Love that you were able to experience this human experience, even as awful as it may feel. Tell that experience and piece of you "I am right here with you and you will never be alone." Tell that piece of you how strong it is to go through this and how grateful you are for its strength. Tell that piece of you that you will never abandon it and that it is safe. Tell it that every part of that experience was to evolve you into a whole new level. This is part of the human experience no matter how horrible it is and feels. This is a gift we have given ourselves to evolve the soul of understanding and feeling in human form. Without that you could not feel the happiness and bliss because once again there would be nothing to contrast it with. This allows you to fully embody living in the moment of bliss because now you know what it feels like to be on the other end. You need this so that you can experience and express yourself. As this may sound harsh, this is the choice that we all chose to create this human experience on this earth. As I said previously, it is an experience and experiment. It was not meant to destroy, but with destruction comes rebuilding and recreating. That is what the mission is now.

We all know what the dark feels like. We know what all the skeletons and shadows feel like. Release them by loving them and thanking them for being part of your life. As you release that heaviness it opens up for the expansion of lightness, blissfulness and joy on a level that you can never imagine. Due to your denseness in this body, you have not experienced it yet. That is what is being created now. The new transition of this world. So that now with fully opened eyes you can see, feel, experience sensations and everything about being in a human body to live out this blissfulness and harmony and be one with all.

When it comes to releasing the mind, it's a little trickier. As human beings have been programmed to believe that everything is from the mind. The mind has taken over. It has become its own thing, a strong muscle. Just like if you were to only work out one leg and not the other, that leg would be way stronger. That's the same concept. The mind has been working out and working out for generations, so it is a much stronger mind, just like that stronger leg, then your heart. Where the heart is the true mind of the being, each being.

Now it's time to allow the muscle in the mind to rest, kind of sit on the couch. Be a bit of a couch potato. Allow the muscle to atrophy a little. You will not become braindead, not all functioning, or not be smart. It's just not going to be the center of everything anymore. What you are gonna do is put your heart on that treadmill or whatever it is to strengthen that muscle, so it becomes the dominant muscle. As you continue to strengthen the heart muscle and it becomes the center, bring that heart muscle all the way down through your entire body into the earth. Then bring it back up into your being. With all aspects of your being's energy, you bring it back up into the heart. As the energy is back into your heart, it now goes up through your voice and through your mind. That muscle is now utilized in a proper way. Utilize the will of the heart. The heart will not deceive. The heart will not make up, overanalyze, or destroy all that is possible. This is the way of living through your power center which is your heart, your voice, and your mind.

We always get hung up with the idea that it is enough to just drop it down into the heart and that is as far as you go. No, drop it through the entire being of your body. The heart is the strength, but it takes the whole unit to create the repatterning, the new creation, and the bliss of what life can be. Allow this now. Feel into this now. Drop your mind, this beautiful mind. Tell it how much you love your mind. Drop it down into the heart. If the heart feels scared or skittish, reassure it that it is strong, it is not alone because you are right there with it. Tell it you are growing together as one. Breathe into it and allow the heart to expand. Bring all thoughts into it. Continue dropping those thoughts all the way down into the pelvic region. Breathe it into the pelvic region creating a figure eight "8" infinity sign. This is your grounding point. Then you drop it straight out of the pelvis through the tailbone into the earth, like you are driving a stake into the ground. Breathe it into the earth. Then you bring that energy back up through, from the earth, through all your aspects and layers of being. Back into your pelvis. Back into your heart. Through your voice. Through your mind and then create. This will create your center. This will create your power in your stability and grounding of creating. Creating this world into the beauty you choose it to be. Take a deep breath into that. Feel it. Know it and expand it. Beautiful! This is the beginning.

RECEIVE

*R*eceiving is a very important aspect that you all need to understand. Receiving does not mean taking from others. Receiving is allowing. Allowing an energy to come through you on a level that you've never experienced. Receiving is simply surrendering into the highest vibration possible that your body can hold. So that you may flow. Allow through and give out without actually giving. Receiving is receiving all the energy that is in this universe with the ability to continue on your journey without it depleting you. When you're not in the receiving mode your body will be depleted very easily by doing, doing - getting, getting - trying, trying - whatever it is that you are doing on a daily level for yourself. Receiving allows the energies to completely flow through the body with ease without trying or doing, just being and being in a surrendered mode. All the energy flowing around you and out of you is also received by others. This energy is important so that you can maintain your stability in your energetic level without feeling wiped out, getting sick, just giving in, feeling drained or crumpled.

To be in the receiving mode is the single most gift that we can give you of purity, clarity, and moving forward. Allow your body to receive now. Open up energetically on the top of your head. Allow this energy to be penetrated into you now. Do not do anything, just surrender. Simply say, "I allow myself to surrender into all that is and to receive, receive, receive bringing forward all that I am." As you receive your body will fill with energy. You will feel like you're on a cloud relaxing. Then as you step forward into your day of whatever it is you feel you need to do or create, this energy allows you to flow with ease, creativity, simplicity of fun and you're not having to do anything. When you're in your receiving mode life is simple and it just flows with ease. No longer going against the grain or up the river. It's simply you flowing as the wave versus you trying to catch the wave.

When you're in a receiving, receptive mode your heart will feel full. You're always in the present moment. Your senses are fully open. You're not going to receive negative things unless you open up your boundaries to allow that. When you go into the receiving mode be sure to always ask for "only the highest vibration." So that your cells in your body may continually hold those higher vibrations and you will continue to grow with this receiving. Do not be concerned that you will receive too much as we know how to regulate it for you and each individual. We will not blow your system out or harm your body. This is simply opening up to the pure channel that each one of you are. Receiving is not only an energy that you will feel fulfilled with but, you also get clarity of your own particular abilities, psychic abilities, and channeling. You will receive clear information that is necessary for you to continue on your path to become the master of who you are. Allow the receiving now. Breath it in with ease. Relax it out. Know that you are the wave. Know that all is possible when you surrender and allow yourself to be the receiver. That you no longer have to be a giver, mustering up all the energy that you have to be able to give, give, give. Receiving is what you were meant to be so you may hold the vibration that transitions you, this earth, and all those around you. You are a receiver. Choose this now for yourself.

AFTERWORD

We thank you for all your time and opportunity for the growth you're allowing yourself. Know that each step you make is one step closer of loving not only yourself but, the world around you. We are always here and you can always call upon us for understanding and up-leveling so that you can continue your growth. You are never alone. Do not worry that you're over asking as this is our duty for each individual on this Earth. Now is the time to grow into the power you are so you will no longer be enslaved by anything, anyone, or yourself. Look for the second book of the series "Light Beam" We thank you and have a beautiful, beautiful experience.

ABOUT THE AUTHOR

*C*orynthia is here to bring forward the teachers and lightworkers of the 5th Dimension and the unfolding New World. *Your True Essence* is her first book, and part of a channeled series, *Frequencies of the New World*.

As a Soul Ascender, Corynthia has the unique skills to guide human souls into their individual, true power. She channels divine one on one teachings with the help of each individual's personal guides and angels as well as her own galactic helpers. She assists the healers, lightworkers and starseeds of the new paradigm to step into their soul purpose and confidently become the new teachers of the 5th dimension.

She works with conscious seekers of all ages and locations through virtual sessions and in person events. Corynthia places a special emphasis on performing channeled healing sessions for groups of all sizes. If you're ready to step into your true evolution of healing and creating, Corynthia is available at http://www.soulascender.com.